CANZONE ITALIANA

CONTENTS

— PIANO LEVEL —
LATE INTERMEDIATE/EARLY ADVANCED

ISBN 978-1-61780-541-7

7777 W. BLUEMOUND RD. P.O. BOX 13819 MILWAUKEE, WI 53213

In Australia Contact:
Hal Leonard Australia Pty. Ltd.
4 Lentara Courst
Cheltenham, 3192 Victoria, Australia
Email: ausadmin@halleonard.com.au

Visit Hal Leonard Online at
www.halleonard.com

Visit Phillip at
www.phillipkeveren.com

CARNIVAL OF VENICE

By JULIUS BENEDICT
Arranged by Phillip Keveren

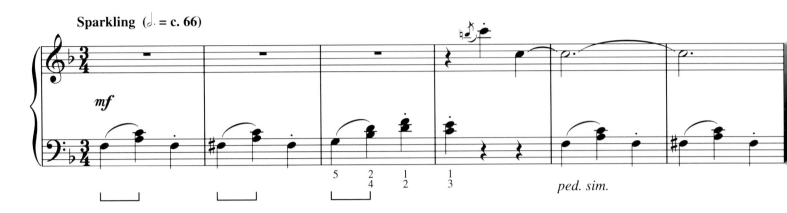

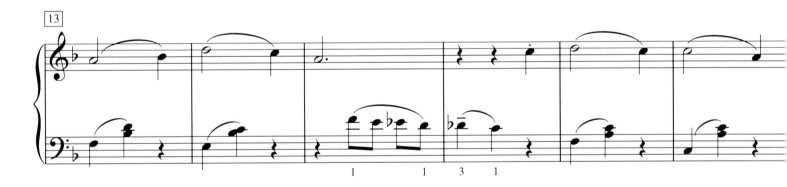

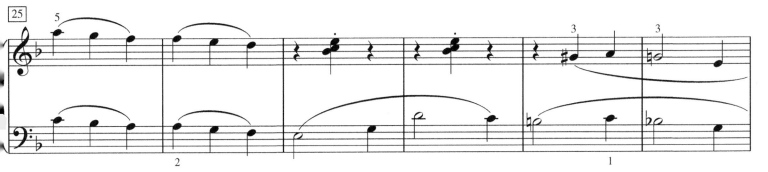

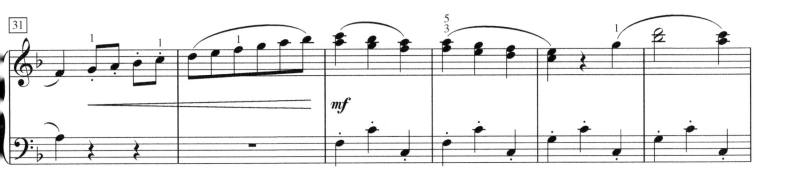

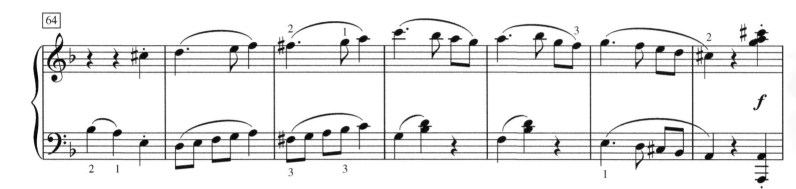

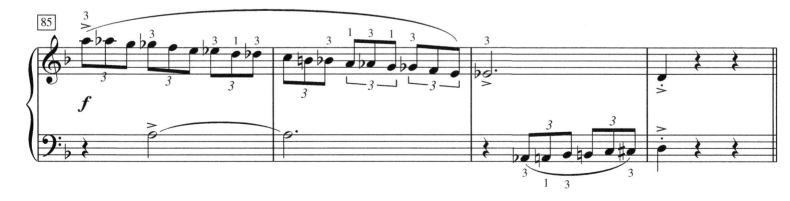

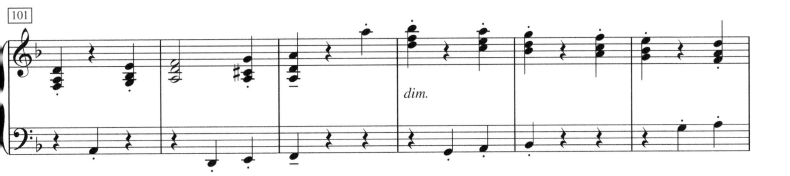

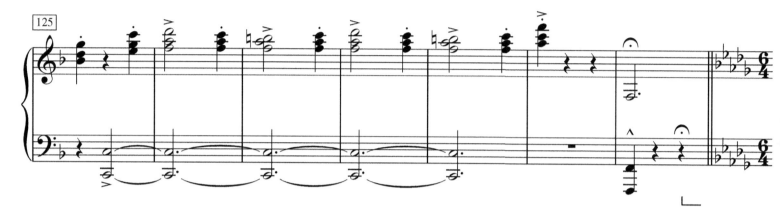

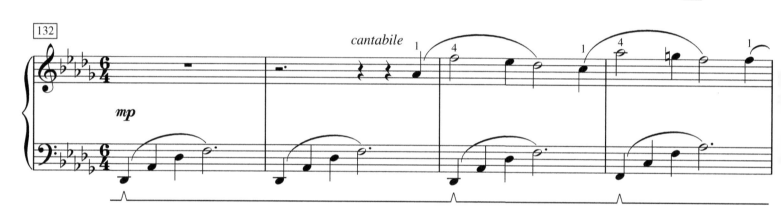

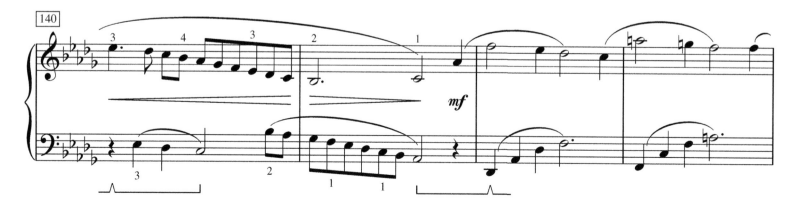

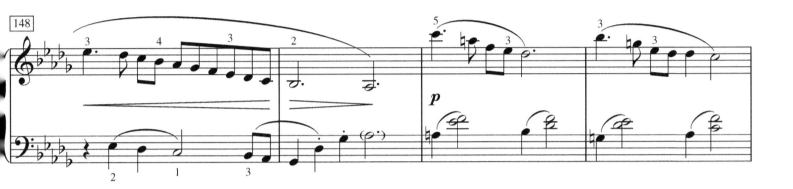

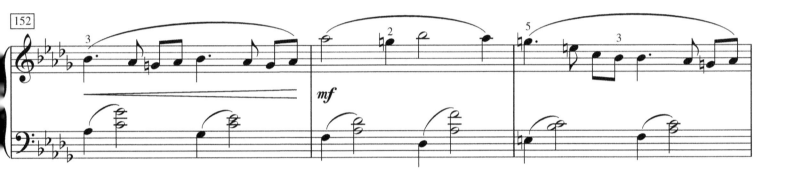

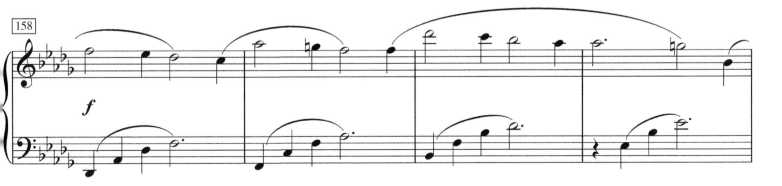

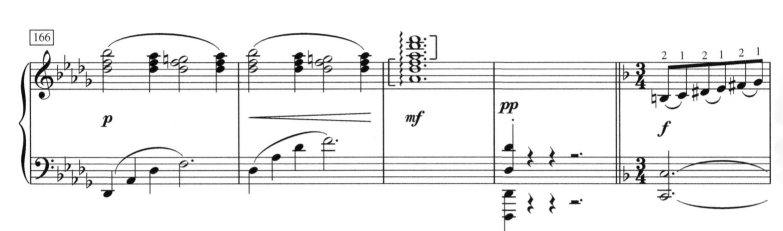

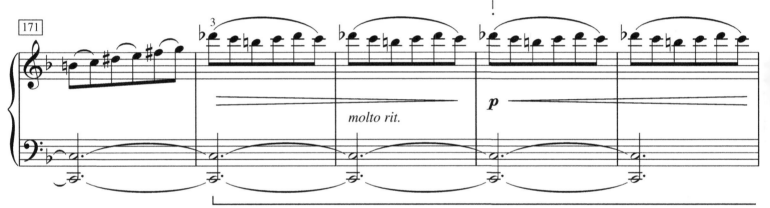

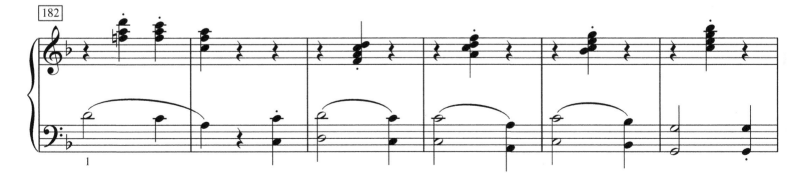

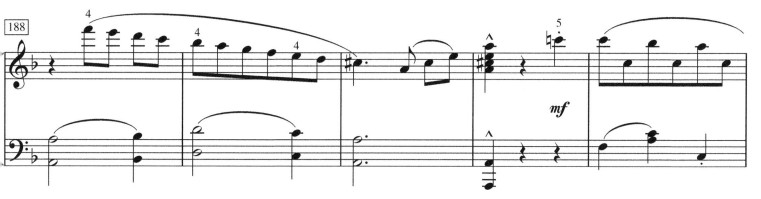

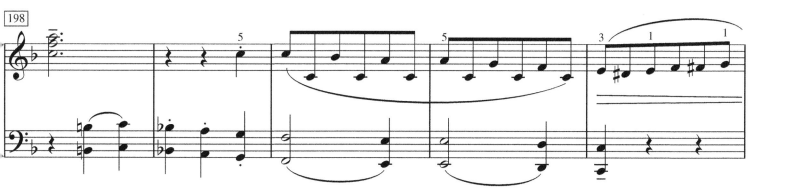

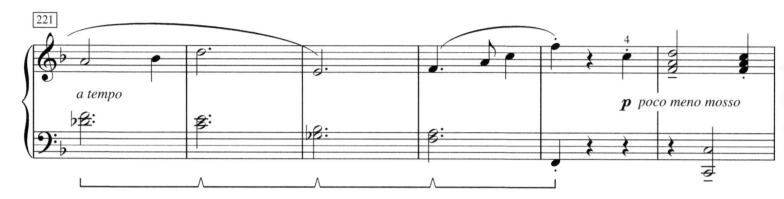

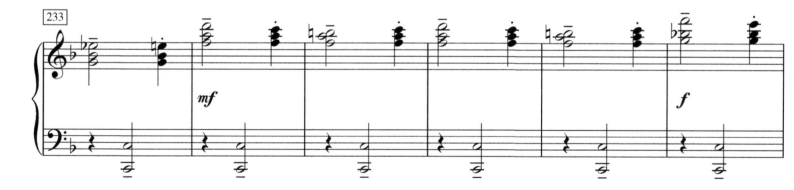

CIRIBIRIBIN

Words and Music by
ANTONIO PESTALOZZA
Arranged by Phillip Keveren

Tempo di Valse (♩ = 192)

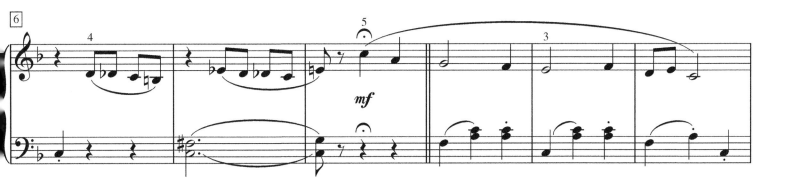

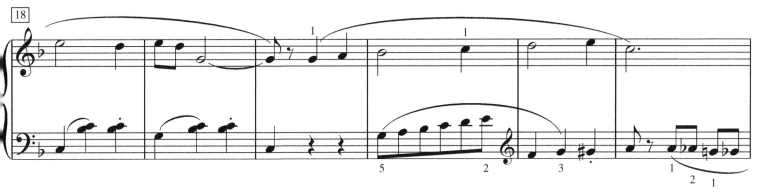

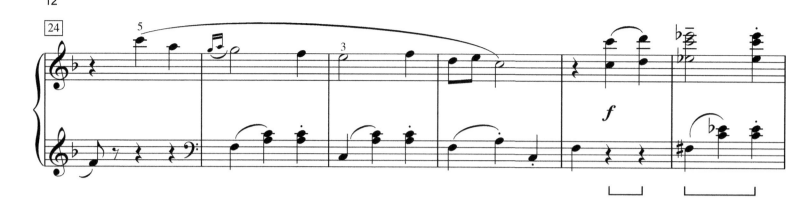

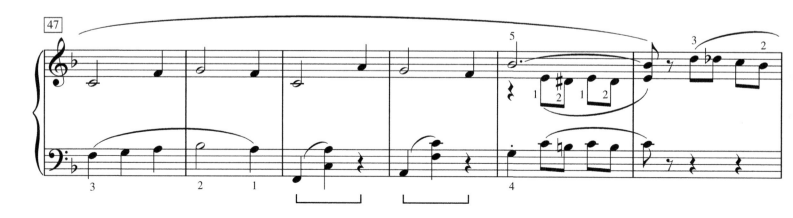

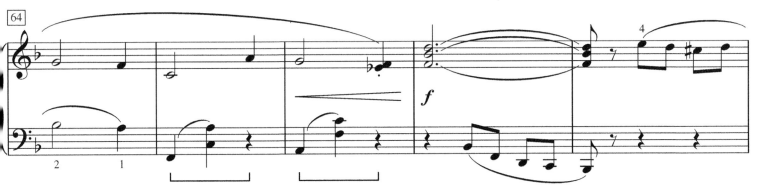

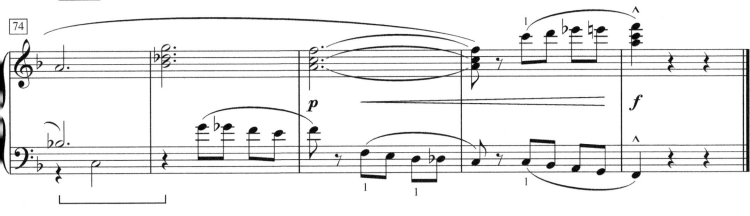

DANCE OF THE HOURS

from LA GIOCONDA

By AMILCARE PONCHIELLI
Arranged by Phillip Keveren

Leggerissimo con grazia (♩ = 152)

poco rit.   *a tempo*

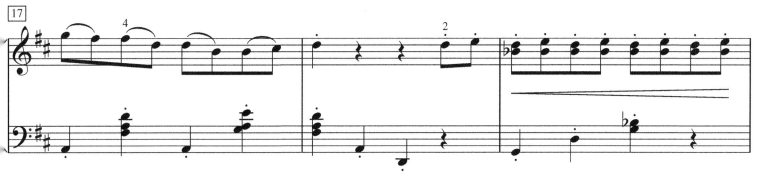

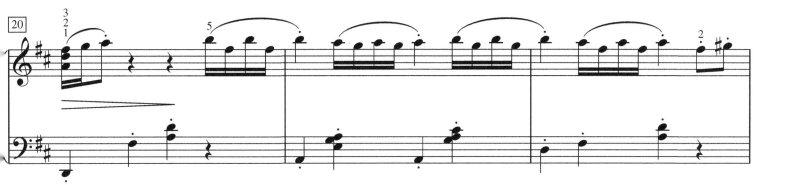

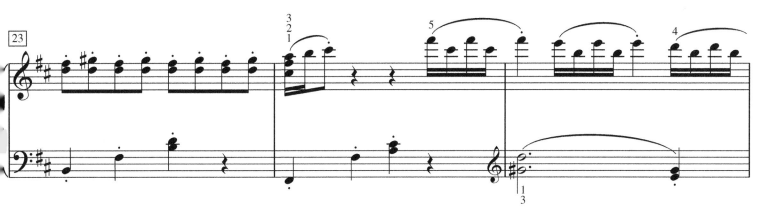

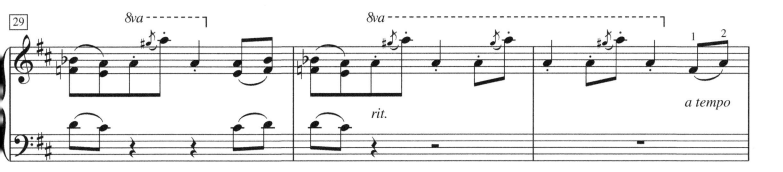

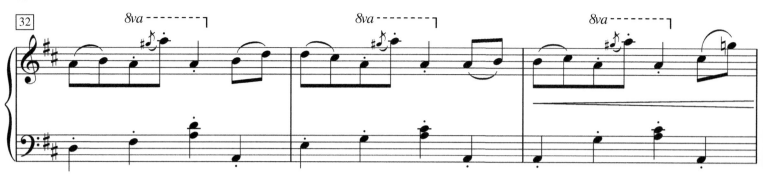

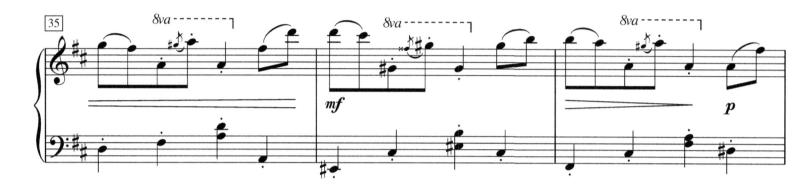

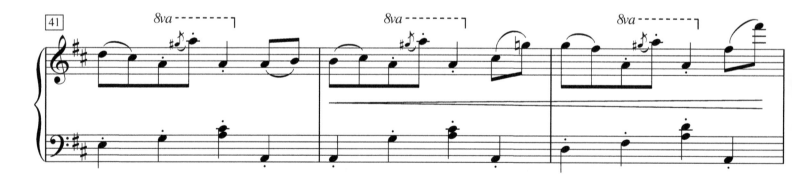

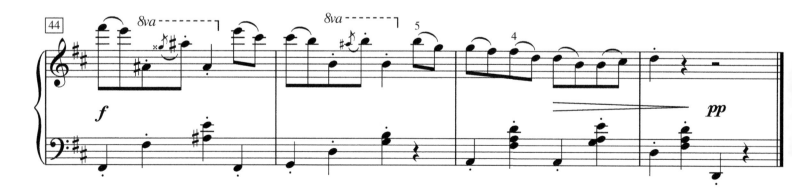

FRATELLI D'ITALIA
(Italian National Anthem)

Words by GOFFREDO MAMELI
Music by MICHELE NOVARO
Arranged by Phillip Keveren

Maestoso (♩ = 120)

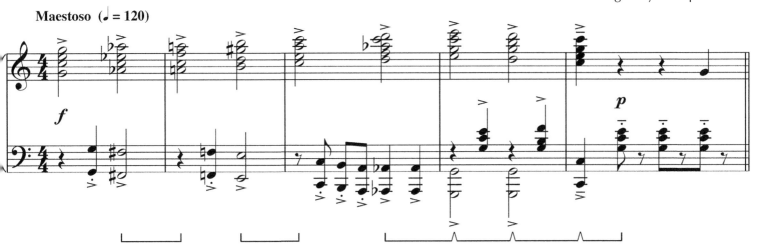

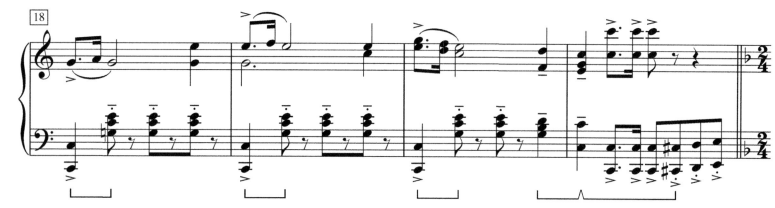

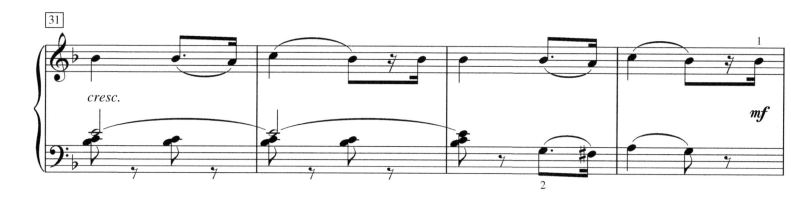

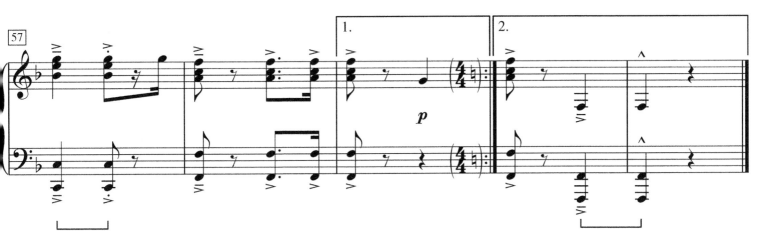

FUNICULI, FUNICULA

Words and Music by
LUIGI DENZA
Arranged by Phillip Keveren

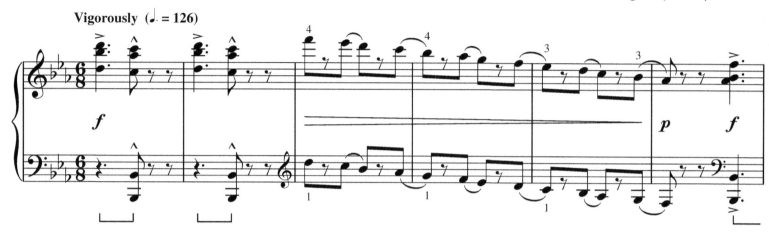

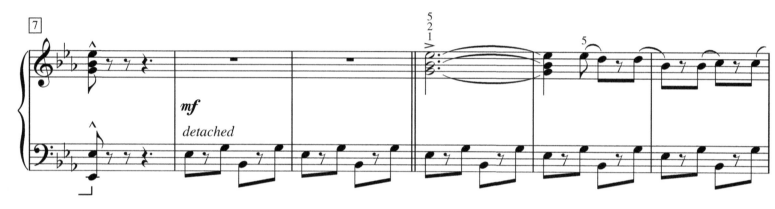

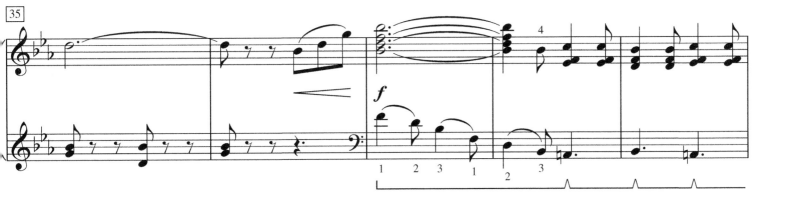

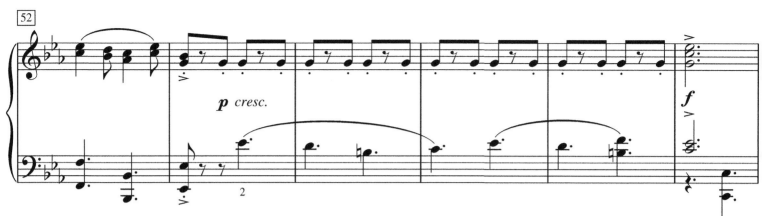

IDEALE

Words by CARMELO ERRICO
Music by FRANCESCO PAOLO TOSTI
Arranged by Phillip Keveren

Expressively, with rubato ($\quarternote = 66$)

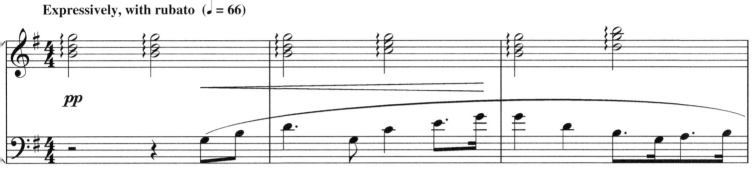

With pedal

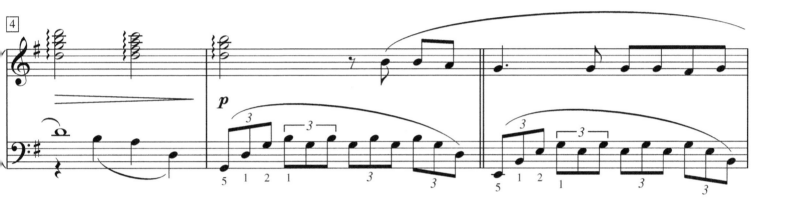

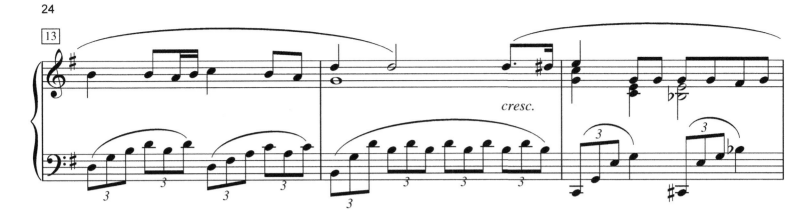

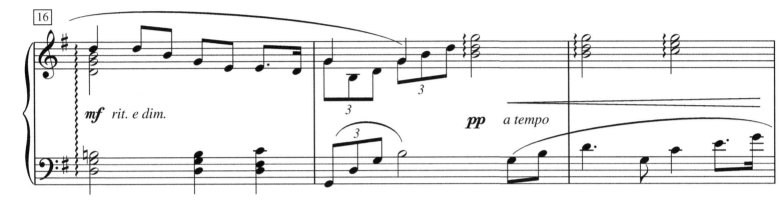

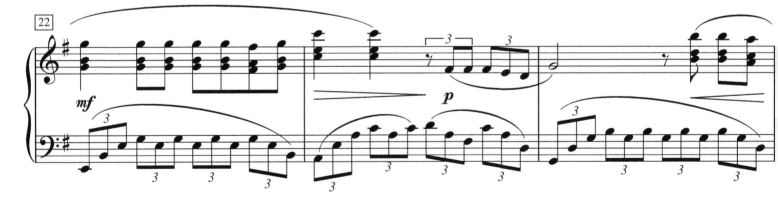

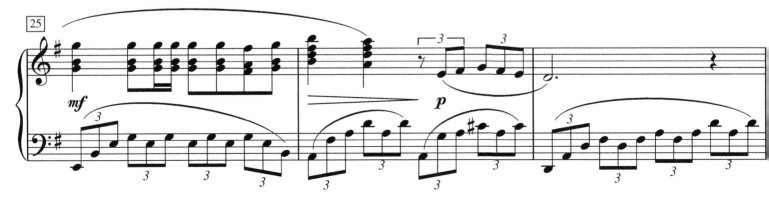

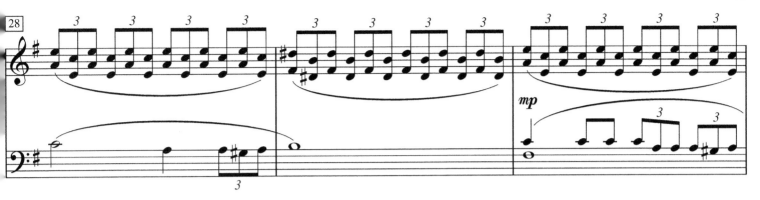

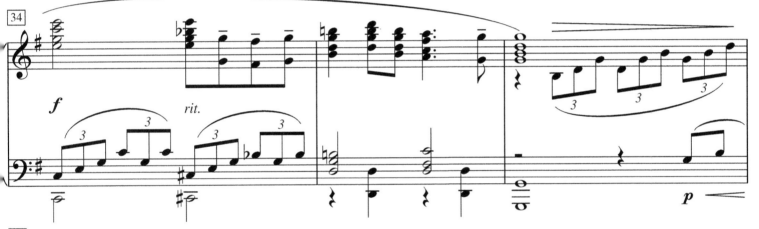

INTERMEZZO
from CAVALLERIA RUSTICANA

By PIETRO MASCAGNI
Arranged by Phillip Keveren

Andante sostenuto (♩ = 56)

With pedal

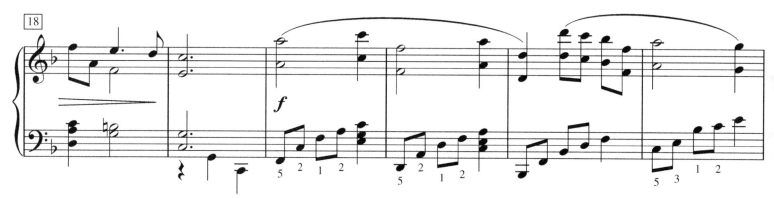

LA DONNA È MOBILE
from RIGOLETTO

By GIUSEPPE VERDI
Arranged by Phillip Keveren

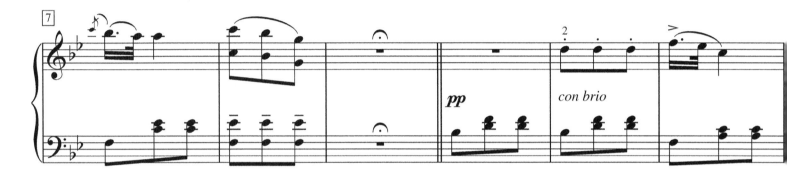

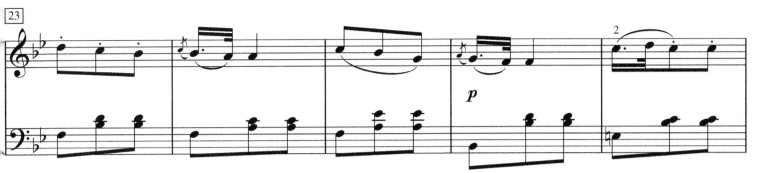

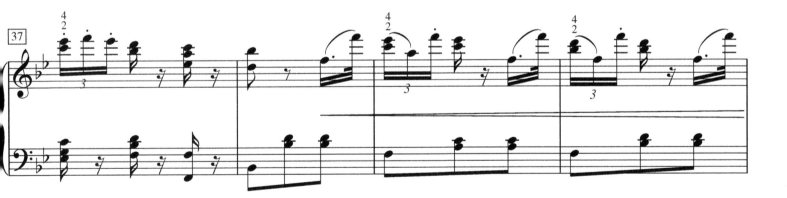

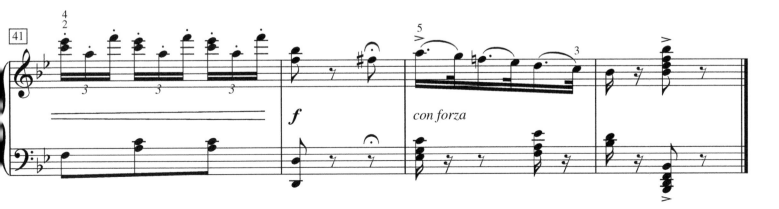

O MIO BABBINO CARO
from GIANNI SCHICCHI

By GIACOMO PUCCINI
Arranged by Phillip Keveren

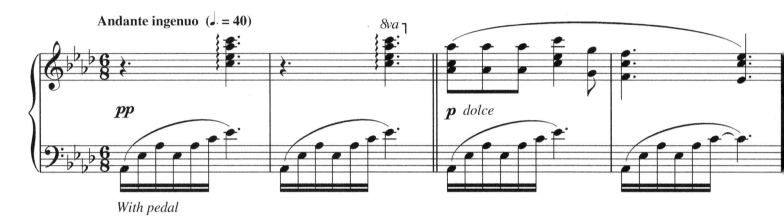

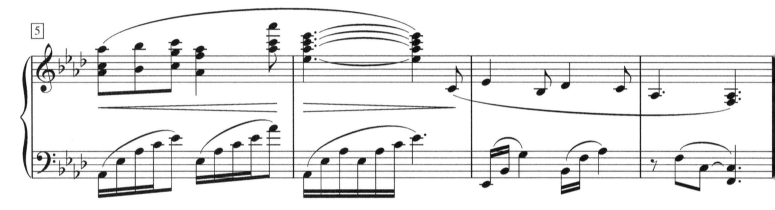

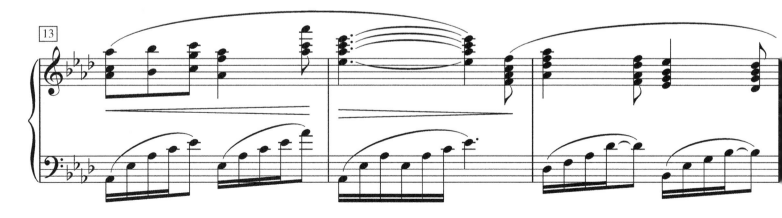

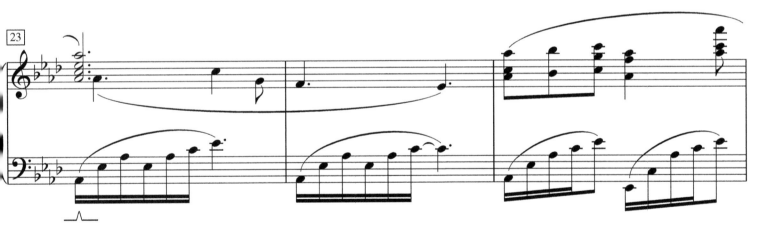

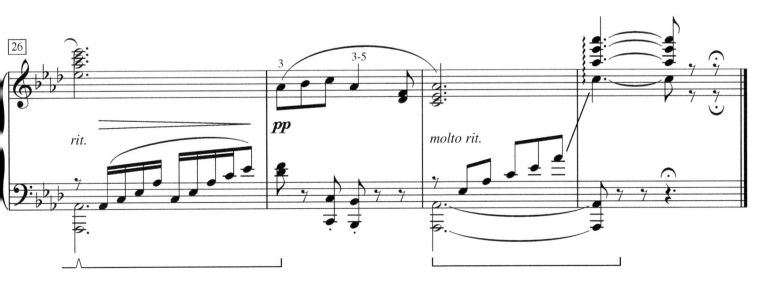

'O SOLE MIO

Words by GIOVANNI CAPURRO
Music by EDUARDO Di CAPUA
Arranged by Phillip Keveren

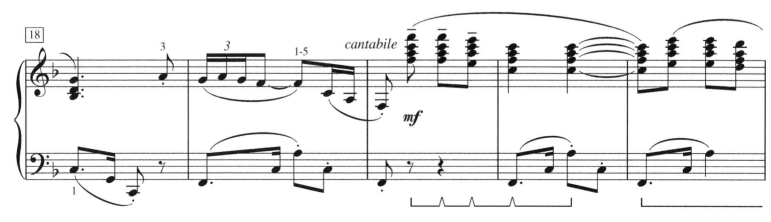

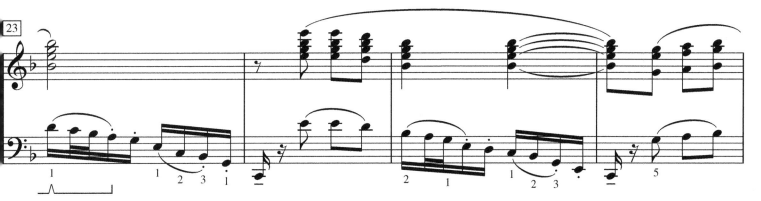

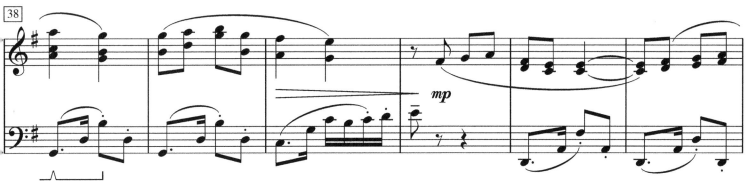

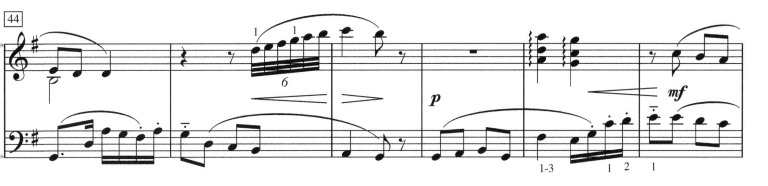

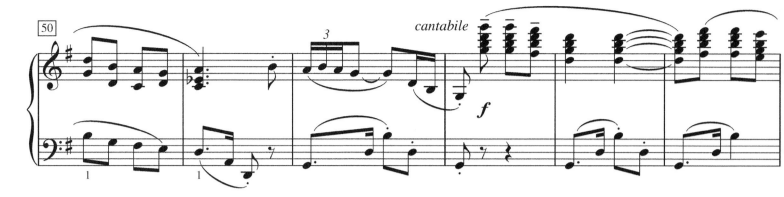

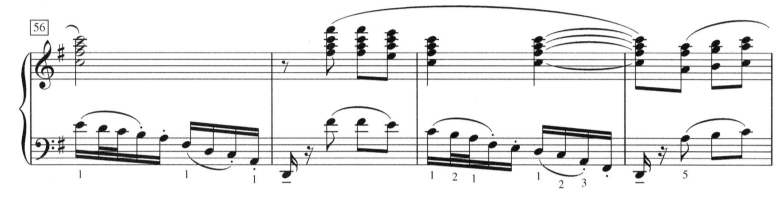

OH MARIE

Words and Music by
EDUARDO DiCAPUA
Arranged by Phillip Keveren

Yearning, with rubato ($\quad$ = 108–112)

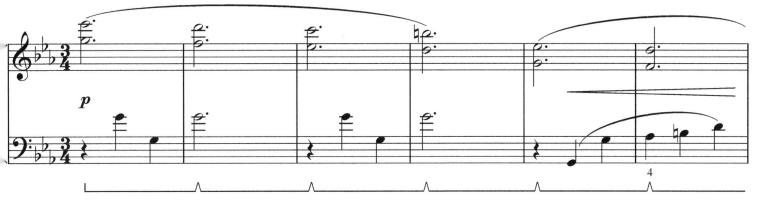

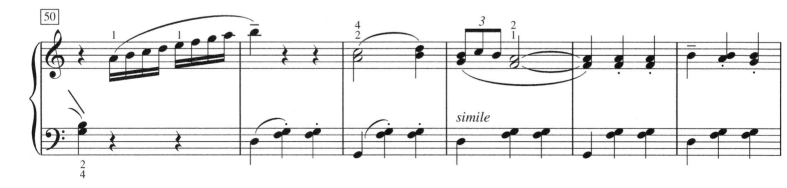

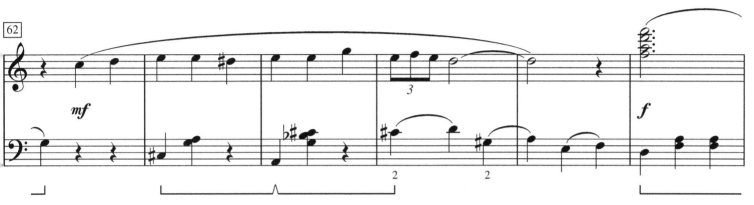

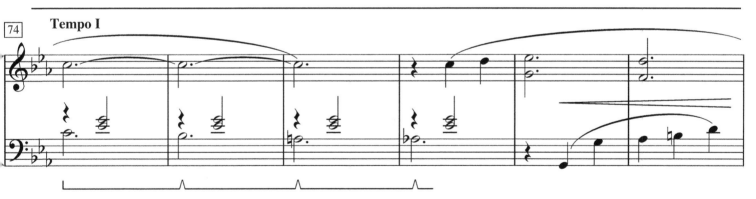

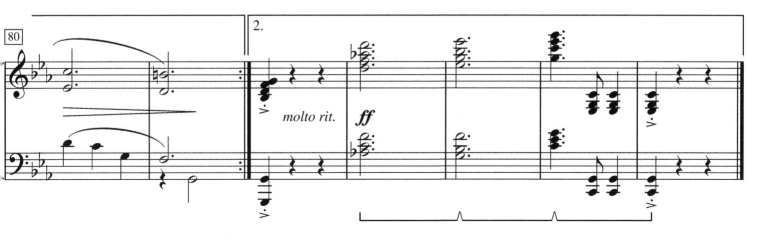

QUANDO MEN VO
(Musetta's Waltz)
from LA BOHÈME

Words by GIUSEPPE GIACOSA
and LUIGI ILLICA
Music by GIACOMO PUCCINI
Arranged by Phillip Keveren

Slowly, with great freedom (♩ = 80)

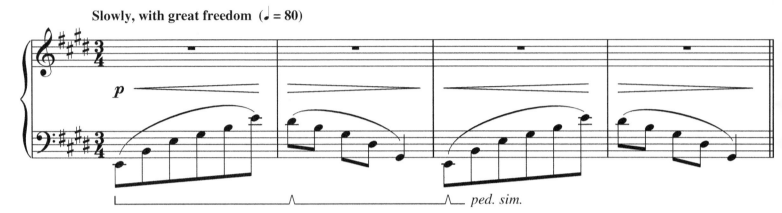

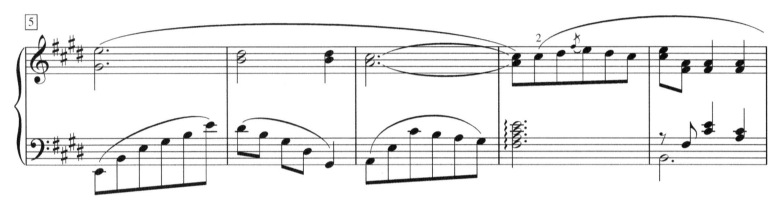

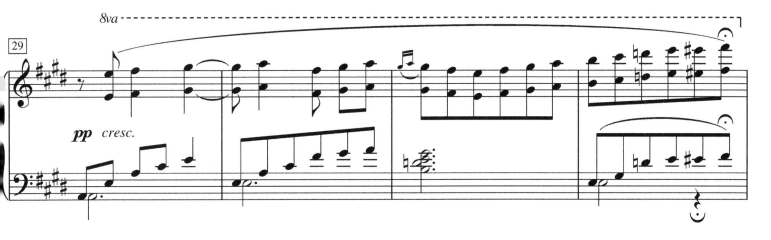

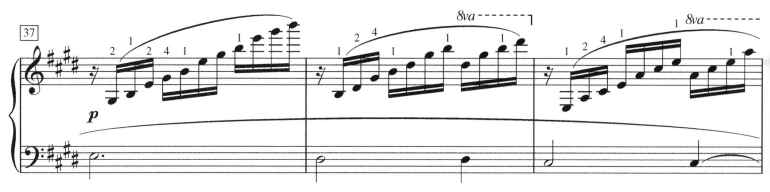

SANTA LUCIA

By TEODORO COTTRAU
Arranged by Phillip Keveren

Tenderly (♩ = 100)

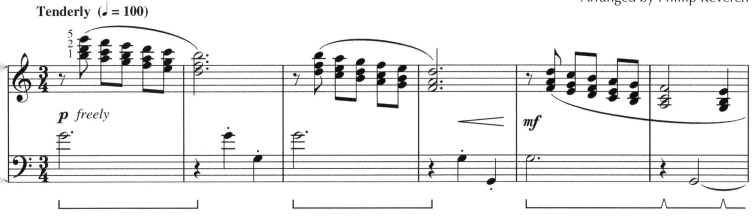

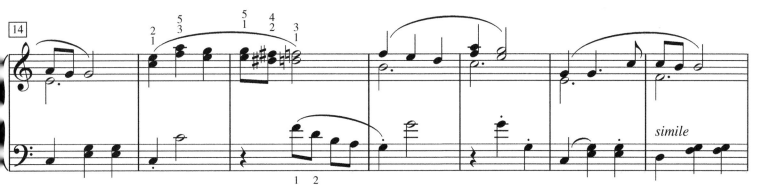

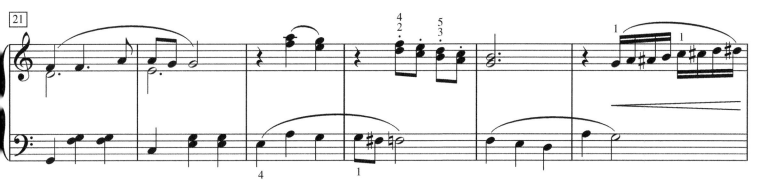

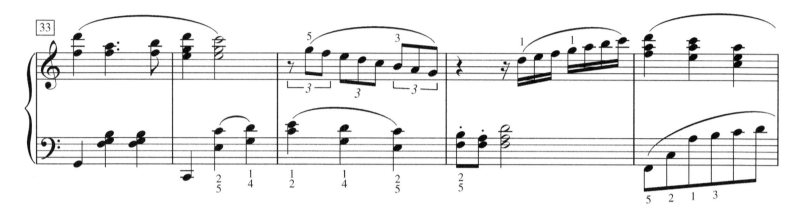

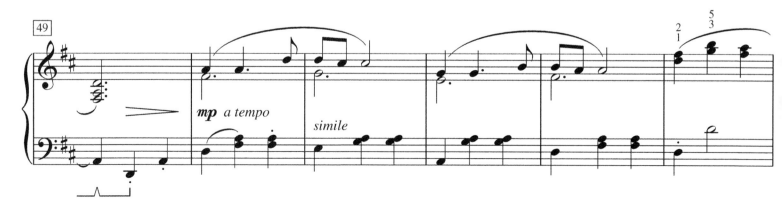

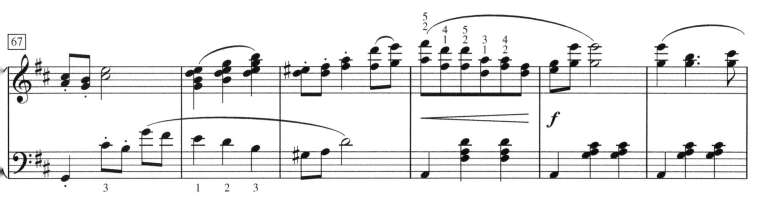

TORNA A SURRIENTO
(Come Back to Sorrento)

By ERNESTO De CURTIS
Arranged by Phillip Keveren

Passionately, with rubato (♩ = 108)

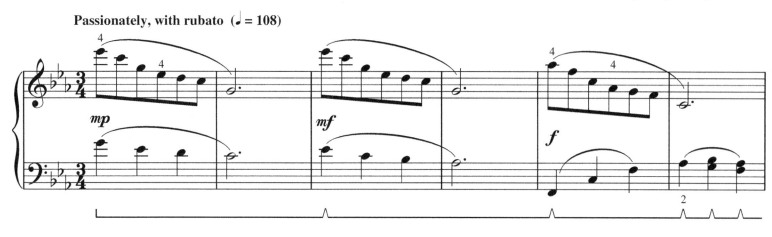

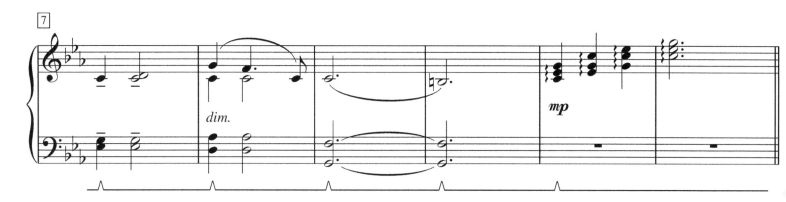

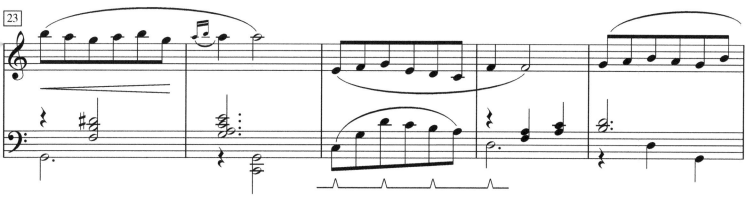

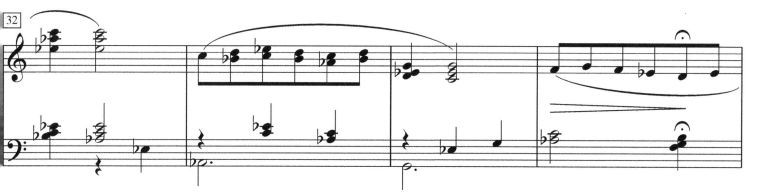

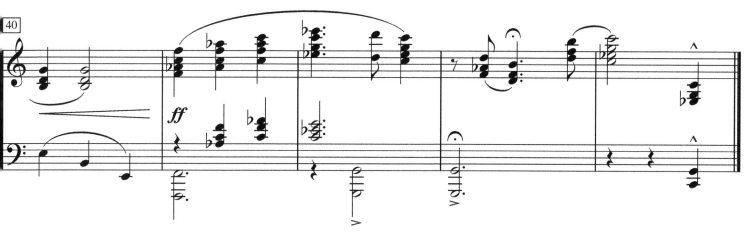

VIENI SUL MAR
(Come to the Sea)

Italian Folksong
Arranged by Phillip Keveren

Flowing Waltz ($\quad$ = 168–176)

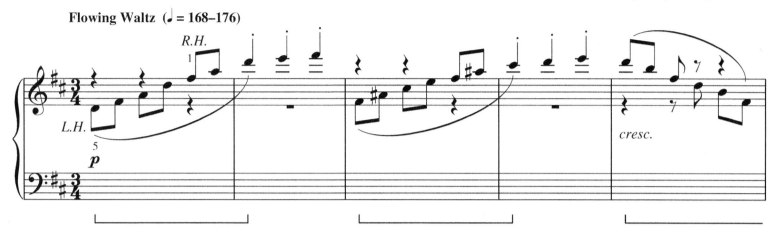

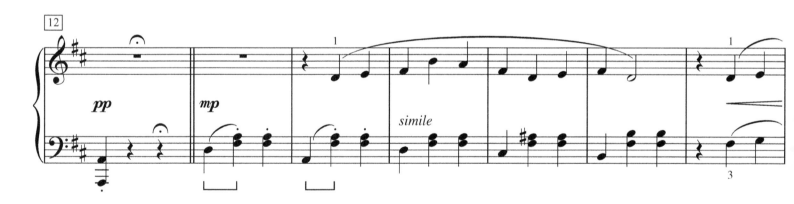

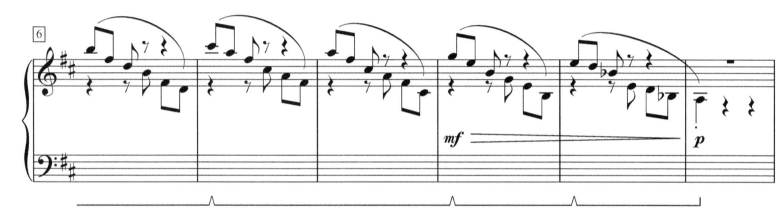

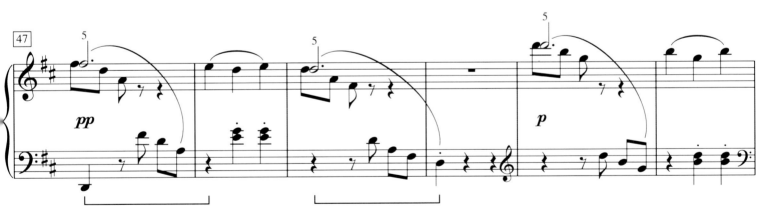

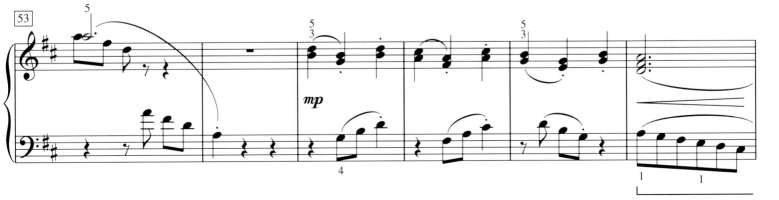

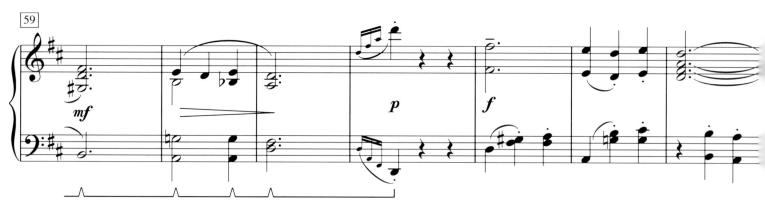

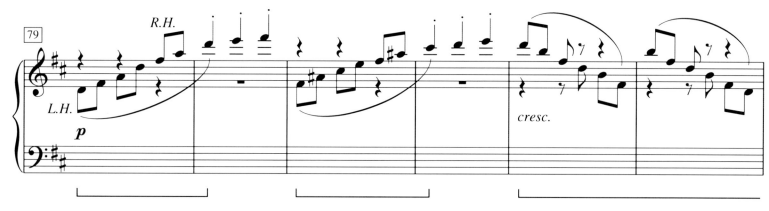